NOTHING REMAINS THE SAME

Tonya Mitchell

The Gap Closer™

A Gap Closer™ Publication
Life On Purpose Publishing
An Angela Massey Imprint

SAN ANTONIO, TEXAS

NOTHING REMAINS THE SAME

A Gap Closer ™ Publication
>A Division of Life On Purpose Publishing
>San Antonio, Texas

Nothing Remains the Same/Tonya Mitchell
ISBN: 978-0-9961908-9-3
Library of Congress Control Number: 2018903610

In loving memory of my grandfather,
Louis Van (L.V.) Montjoy, Sr.
(1920–2014)

ACKNOWLEDGEMENTS

I WOULD LOVE to give a great big 'THANK YOU!" to my biggest supporters of all:

- Murlee and Ronald Pulley, my parents
- Tyianna Davis
- Tyra Bonner
- Carlos Nelson

To all my family and friends with a few shout outs to a few people that always said I could do this:

- Dr. Angela Massey, my editor and publisher
- Uncle Roy Lee Mitchell
- Laurie Mitchell
- Thelma Madison
- LaToya Ware

- Altony Clark
- J.W. Nelson
- A'Dgereanna and Robert Armor
- Sylvia Jones
- Marion and J.T. Buxton
- Irene and Jerry Mitchell
- Archie "Butch" Mays
- Raquel Nelson
- Ashley Mitchell
- Tyeshia Mitchell
- Marcus Dixon, Jr.
- Viola Blow
- Mary and William Glasper
- Joan and Larry Quinn
- Dorion Davis
- Pat and Noble Nelson
- Towanda Liggins
- Tonia Harden
- Varnie Edwards
- Ora Bell
- Pat Washington
- Jessie Lane
- Global Vista Travel
- Francis Rucker
- Janet Green
- Lillie and William Stoudermire Jr

- Zenobia Stevens
- Beverly and Tom Oliver
- Rita Savage
- Ron Mitchell Sr
- Marilyn Renfro
- Stacey Bohnert
- Shelia Mitchell
- Johna Harris
- Idell and Curtis Bean
- Robert and Penny Mitchell
- Jessie Mae Mitchell
- Wilma Mitchell
- Bridget and Melvin Williams
- Helen and Rodney Baker
- Leona Yarber Burkley
- Lenora and Johnny White
- Brad Pickett
- Larry Holloway
- Bill Bolten
- Tom Kniestedt
- Rich Stephens
- Kenny Bradshaw
- Rob Hale
- Virgie and Limmie D. Pulliam
- Brianca Johnson
- Lisa Kay
- Ralph Wannabaker

- Fred Flook
- John Gileselman
- Carey Wunderlich
- Dorothy and Bobby Bennett
- Ed Meadows
- Ronald and Jessica Pulley
- Roshonda Pulley
- Tanecia Pulley
- Brenda Lewis
- Unity District COGIC
- All the clients from Murl's Touch
- The Senior Citizens on the Move
- Church family (Christ Sanctuary COGIC)

In memory of a special friend: Ms. Ruth Newton

In memory of my cousin, Lisa Y. Lane, who told me I should put the stories into a book.

Much love to my grandson, Dorion Akeem Davis Jr and my granddaughter, Brooklyn Royell Davis.

DEDICATION

I dedicate this book to Grandpa. If you were still here, you would love this book. Thank you for encouraging me to do this. I appreciate you giving me your journal and trusting me with your story. I love you forever more.

CONTENTS

INTRODUCTION

REMEMBER WE either grow old or die young. So, one day, hopefully, the younger generation will at least have a person like me. I don't say that to brag or boast. I say it because I love senior citizens and I believe as we age, there should be at least one person in our life who cares about our well-being. I have chosen to be that person for many of the seniors in Sikeston, Missouri.

This book is written in two parts. The first part is the journal of my beloved grandpa. I promised him that I would publish it, and this is that promised fulfilled. I have not altered the language or made any grammatical corrections. These are his words the way he penned them.

My grandpa was a guy who had a lot to say. Grandpa was a man of his word. Once you met him, there's no way you would forget him. He has often said, "I have done everything in my life, but kill a white man." (Thank God!) To my knowledge, he has never met a stranger. Grandpa was full of love, laughter, education, and wisdom.

He was that guy who believed in education and he did all he could do to make sure he got his education. Back when he was school-aged it was unheard of for black folks to graduate from high school, because they had no choice but to go to the cotton fields.

You couldn't tell Grandpa anything because as he would always say, he was like an old refrigerator, he couldn't keep nothing!

He was as honest as they came, and he always said he didn't see any sense about lying because you definitely were going to get caught sooner or later. Even though being honest could get people's feelings hurt, he just couldn't help but to "tell it like it is."

Writing this book was supposed to be our journey. Grandpa told me one day to do it. Even though I'm just getting started, I never gave up Grandpa's vision. He saw something, and he knew one day it would get done. If it wasn't for him, pushing me, I don't think I would have ever had the desire.

The second part is about my adventures with a group of senior citizens, and Grandpa was an important member of that group.

I believe honoring senior citizens is a must. If we take an honest look at our lives—the things we as black folk enjoy: owning our homes, being able to vote, being able to work and play as we choose— if it wasn't for them, we wouldn't exist, and our lives would not be what they are today.

It's a blessing how God gave them the mind to be able to teach and show their children how to succeed in this world. It's something how a lot of the seniors didn't get past the second grade but could read and write.

My Senior group was full of laughter, love, and wisdom They liked to have fun. They chose to make the best of every moment they had left. And in this book, I share a few of the road trips and other activities we were able to enjoy together.

Seniors deserve recognition and honor for the remarkable lives they've lived, the struggles they've overcome, and the raising and teaching they have provided. So, this book was written to give them exactly that.

Tonya Mitchell
Sikeston, Missouri

Part 1:

Grandpa's

Journal

CHAPTER ONE

MEET MR. L.V. MONTJOY

MY NAME is L.V. Montjoy. I was born April 27, 1920 in Wolf Island, Missouri. You know where that is, south of East Prairie? Do you know where Ringo Store is, southeast of East Prairie? Okay. Let me tell you a little bit about my history.

After all these years my first real memory is when I was a kid, about three years old, and my granny took a picture of me leaning up against a tree. I didn't have any hair because she shaved all my hair off. I still got the picture now. After that, I grew up—let me skip about three or four years.

My Daddy

My daddy moved to Ringo Farm at Wolf Island in 1928. That was the same year he made plenty money—he got $9.75 a week—and he bought a Model-T or 28' Chevy for a couple hundred dollars from Mitchell Sharp Chevrolet Company in Sikeston.

I had an uncle named Sydney. He called my daddy "Dick" and asked Daddy to take him to the doctor. Well somebody had something against my daddy and threw a brick in his car. It hit Uncle Sidney in the face after having all his teeth pulled and my daddy didn't like that. No, he didn't like that.

Daddy stopped at home and woke me up. See, he carried a gun and I had one too, and if he got high I would have his gun and mine too. We went to this guy's house and parked the car on the bank of the levy where the lights shined down to his house. I told my dad, "See that man; he's got a gun." He said, "That's the same guy that threw the brick in my car and hit Uncle Sidney."

Yes! I was scared to death! This guy pulled his gun and said, "Don't come no further!" My daddy said, "This 38 special will take care of his 45." All at once that 38 started talking and this guy was on the front porch. He ran to the back door and partly fell into the back door. I was so glad he didn't shoot me.

I stayed there all-night long. In those days wherever you fell, you stayed until they had an inquest before they would move the body. I told the police what happened. The police told my dad to go home. I was a brave young man then. I was about 11 years old then.

My daddy didn't care what we done just so we done what they said. My mom's sister, Theresa, lived with us and she thought she was our momma. We all smoked in the barn and when Theresa saw smoke coming from the barn she would get a stick to whip us. Sometimes we would go out in this deep water up to our waist and Theresa would stand on the bank and throw anything in the water just to make it splash in our faces. We would tell her, "If you want some kids to mind, you should have some of your own." That's what our daddy told us.

My daddy was supposed to be an outlaw in those days. A day's work was a dollar a day—you worked from sunup to sundown. We sold liquor for him while he was at work. We sold this white lightning in a coke bottle with a corn cob in it for $1 to people passing by going to the store. The boss man liked my daddy because he was a good worker. In the winter time he would say, "Dick, what kind of meat you want for the winter?" If my daddy said either beef or pork, it was killed.

One day a man named Oat Watson came riding by and said the Revenues was at Story looking for a boot legger. I told Mr. Oat, "Glad you told us." We had eight gallons of white lightning. We put it in the ground where the dogs dug holes under the house where they could go to hide from gnats and flies. When the man came by we had a marble game on top of it. The man searched the house, but he didn't find nothing. We had that stuck down in the ground where the dogs dug where they could hide from the flies. I know you never seen nothing like that. My daddy was scared to come home because the Revenues had ripped him off, but he had kids smart enough to know what was going on. That was in the Great Depression days.

In 1932—you know how women is—they will have a falling out with their husband; I don't know if they got a man on the side or not. My mama started with some other guy. You know how women is…if they see somebody else, they think he's better, whether they got anything or not. She ran off with that guy and went to Canalou, Missouri. That left me and my dad. He picked up a lady named Leona Cotton. She was supposed to be his housekeeper, but she was his woman. Way after a while she had a young'un and named her Lilly Mae Cotton. Back then it wasn't welfare, and she went in her mama's family name. I haven't seen her since the middle 40s. I'd like to see her now. Back then people didn't count half. Then we move from Ringo's back down to Grandpa's.

EDUCATION

In Medley, Missouri, 1934, you went to school probably a couple of days a month. I didn't know anything about school. You went, and you didn't get any grade for it. The teacher, Mabel Webster, use to come by and she would beg us to go to school. If we went she would tell us to sit in the little hay box in the back of her buggy. This church, Mount Zion Baptist Church, was used for school purposes on the Pasman Lane Road. The white teacher would turn out a little early, so the colored kids and the white kids would meet at the same time. So, when we met we would be at the same place to fight.

We had one family of kids, they was kin to our teacher and the teacher was kin to us. We didn't believe they was kin to us because they didn't look like us.

1932 to 1934 in Joe Louis's day, he was 16 then. My teacher and him was the same age. He went to high school with her. She is still living now.

I even had the same teacher in high school in 1934. I was a man and I went to Lincoln School in

Sikeston and Wolf Island. In them days you chopped cotton and picked cotton. You didn't have time for an education, but I'd go to different places at different times. When I started school in Sikeston in 1932 I had a future of education. I was in the second grade. Just think, 12 years old and you are ready to get out of school. But now you graduate from high school and you might be on the sixth-grade level. When I finished grade school in 1936 I was 16. In 1936 I got a diploma. In 1936 here come the flood and my diploma was in the flood. It still got the water marks on it now. Do you want to see it now?

In this flood we lost everything we had except two horses. We rode them 26 miles in 10° below freezing rain. When I got to Charleston my folks were looking for me. When they found me they put me to bed to get warm. I stayed in the bed three days and nights. I could hear them talking, but I couldn't say anything. The doctor said I was frozen.

My teacher, Hazel Eutingburg, when school was out she brought my diploma down on Tom Brown's farm to me. Tom Webster was the overseer of the farm where we was picking cotton. Snow was on the ground ½ knee deep where we were pulling cotton for $1.00 a hundred pounds. The hulls have to freeze open or you beat them open. This lady brought it to me in the field.

That year we had 75 kids in one room and that year 13 graduates. All was kin to me except one. We didn't like him because he didn't look like us. Man, prejudice been around a long time. You don't know what I'm talking about when I say he didn't look like us. I'm talking about Aunt Ira but her kids weren't kind to me. Ha ha! But they all was kin to Granny. That's funny to be like that, ain't it? They was kin to our greater folks before us.

When I graduated—I was in and out when you chopping cotton in Missouri County. I went to Scott County and went to school. I was thinking about my education and that in nine years I'll be 21 when I graduate. I had a future.

There were three schools in Sikeston. Two white schools (South grand up by Piggly Wiggly) (Tanner Street) one black school Lincoln. Fair-Maud Street. We had a three-room school with three teachers and one principal from the south of Mount Bayou. Ethel Jones, teacher; Lestene Rogers, teacher; Maria Redd, teacher; and Joseph E. Gaines, principal. The principal had a room in the back called the shop. That man was wonderful. Anything you gave him he could make music out of it. Then when you came from the South you was supposed to be educated.

When I graduated from school in Sikeston, they gave me a thing to go to Lincoln school in Charleston in 1938 -1939. I went to Charleston. We didn't have a school bus. I drove a private-owned vehicle belonging to Chevrolet on Malone west of the theater. It belonged to George Whiteheat. I don't know the price of the vehicle. They gave me $.35 a day to do the driving. Man, that was a lot of money! Of course, a driver's license was just $.25 for three years. They did ask if you could ride a bike, which I couldn't. Gasoline was $.25 at Malone's. Whiteheat didn't say when to park his car. I used his car for my convenience. I used it as a cab on weekends. I carry you uptown for a dime cab fare. If you wanted to shop that price was $.25. In 1939, that was the year my brother died. When he was young, he said all that he was going to do when he reached 21. When he got 21 he died. When they had his funeral my mama didn't let me know.

In our last two years in school they showed us a picture called *Gone with the Wind* in a white theater where they didn't allow black folks. This movie was four hours long. After the movie on our way to Sikeston we had a tornado as I drove along the highway. The wind was blowing houses away just in front of us. I drove fast. The kids said, "Why are you driving so fast?" I said, "I want to be in the gone with the wind!" We made the trip safely.

We had two more years to go to finish school the year was 40-41. I graduated from Lincoln in Charleston. Some of the kids—we started school from the second grade until we finished school. Back then you could get all you could for the price of $.35

I saw a girl at her brother's funeral while back at that same school. A lot of days I would buy her dinner and when we got home I would tell her parents what she owed me. They would pay me back.

LIFE IN THE ARMY

When school was out I was 21 years old. Then I started getting these draft letters for the Army. We had a country post office. Miss Trucy would tell me, "L.V., you got some mail." I would take it because I knew what it was. Done that two times, and when I opened it, it said "You will be in Jefferson Barrick, December 7, 1941." I was there that morning Pearl Harbor was bombed. I passed my physical — class A1.

My grandparents was old so the Army let me go back home. They called me again. Said you will be here January 14, 1942 to be sworn in at St. Louis. I got my first 13-week training in Texas. After that, 13 weeks in Shreveport Louisiana. And after that I was sent to Fort Huachuca, Arizona for nearly 2 years and then I went overseas: Guam, Biak, Okinawa, Solomon, New Guinea, all over the South Pacific.

My organization, 93rd Infantry Division, was all black. I spent four years in that organization and a lot of stuff went on in that length of time. We slept on the ground and in foxholes. They gave us a sandwich every third morning about 4 o'clock in the morning with a cup of coffee. In my basic training I had the highest score you could get with a weapon. I made expert. I think that's why they sent me overseas so quickly. Dwight Eisenhower was our leader and he wanted well-trained men in the 93rd division all black.

My first pay was $.70 per day or $21 a month. After a short time, I made two stripes and my pay went to $34 and when I made Sargent, my pay was $78, that's a lot more than $21. I sent my grandma $300 a month. How did I do that? I played cards for money, sold beer, cigarettes, cigars and chewing tobacco. Beer was $1.92 for 24 bottles. My price was a dollar a bottle. Cigarettes, $.50 a carton. My price one dollar a pack. The rest was like wise. I paid for this out of my pocket first, then the profit was mine.

Some days we would go to work at 6 o'clock in the morning and work until 12 o'clock at night unloading war supplies. I was the supply sergeant. So many days I had to do the delivering two different companies. I drove a landing voyage to different posts. One night we went down to the boat deck where you could see plenty fish just like looking in a fish tank. So, we decided wanted some to eat. We put a box of dynamite in the water and killed plenty fish. One came up a big Seabass and it took seven men to carry the fish to our tent. Laying on its side it was high as my shirt pocket. We cooked it in a 5-gallon grease can with four Coleman burners. Just in time it got cooked, an officer arrived. He had us charged with killing fish with dynamite. But that fish was so good he ate some of it. When it came time for him to prosecute, I told he helped us, so he had to drop the charge. I came home with an honorable discharge.

BACK HOME

I'm back home now, it's January 1946. My grandparents still owned their farm, so I got a $300 check from when I got out of the Army. I got me two mules, so I could work the land. I worked 58 acres and rented the rest to other farmers. On my farm we had hogs, chickens, goats, cows, turkeys. I had done pretty good that year trying to get started again. And in 1947 I had a lot of hogs, and four mules. Grandpa died the same year. All my hogs died and three of the mules. This is winter time, so I waited until spring came before buying some more.

I started all over again in 1948 and accumulated my loss back pretty close to what I had before. I would go to work with white shirt, tie, and suit, drive mules all day, take my work clothes off hang them on the wire where I hung my suit. Take a rinse off in the horse drinking water and walk back home. In 1948 I got me some more mules then I could ride to work. I could shuck 100 bushels of corn a day for $20. I shucked for three different farms.

In the winter of 1949 the flood came again. We moved to Charleston, stayed there all winter. I had four mules, one cow, two calves, five pregnant sows, and lots of chickens. My aunt let me put them in her garden. That really was a bad winter. Sows had pigs the coldest night. I would take them in the house to keep them from freezing (that was hard times).

MARRIAGE AND FAMILY

In the spring of 1950 we moved back home, saved all we brought out of the flood and started all over again.

I got married May 16, 1950. I stayed with my grandma until she sold her farm in 1952. I moved in a house that belonged to the man that brought my farm. I went and worked for him as a farmhand for $5 a day.

I moved. I had a wife, one child, two mules, a wagon, and a pig. I went to Wigsdor Furniture got some stuff for my house, beds, dresser, electric stove, refrigerator, deep freezer, and washing machine. My payment was $9.90 a month.

I worked for 12 years on this farm. One day we were getting ready to go to Ducain State Fair to show our cattle. I got ran over with the tractor in front of my house. I had 10 children and my wife was pregnant with twins. The time was June 1964 and I went to the hospital. I stayed until September. My doctor let me come home so I could be home when my twins were born. That night my sister-in-law carried my wife to the hospital—she called back and said you got a girl and a boy. Before they was born the girls wanted another girl, the boys wanted another boy, so when they came I had six boys and six girls…that's still even.

Our phone was 649-2524 on a party line; my ring was one long and one short. Our little dog Chaghuccca Roudy knew the ring. When it rang, he would wake you up.

In 1965 I moved to Charleston. I tried to get a project house, but they told me my family was too big. One guy lived next to the office, he had 22 in one house. I told the Housing Authority about it, but they never did move him out. See how people will do you when you can't help yourself.

I was also crippled. We moved into a big old raggedy house with mostly rats. We burned our lights all night. You could put out a 5-pound box of DeCon at night and the next morning it would all be gone.

In 1966 I moved in a house near Bertrand with free house rent. I fed this man's (Jessie Workman) one sow and 10 pigs once a day. He had some calves. I would go and turn the windmill on to pump the water. Sometimes I would take him to the doctor. My wife helped his daughter keep the house. We done this to show appreciation.

In the spring of 1967 we moved to Sikeston. I still wasn't able to work. My wife went to school and had two or three little jobs. When she finished her schooling, she got a job at the hospital where she worked for 8 ½ years.

This went on until 1969. I got a job as a bus driver for Sikeston Public Schools. All my kids finished high school in Sikeston, some finished college. I drove from 1969 to 1983. During this time, I also cut grass. I mowed grass during spring and summer and in the fall I raked leaves. In the winter time I shoveled snow. I kept a job the year round. I accumulated 42 yards. The first yard I got in 1972 and I'm still cutting it now. During this time, I had another girl born May 15, 1971.

In 1983, the school took my job. I didn't mind it too much. That gave me all my time for my yards. I made much more money than I got from the school. I averaged $350 per week with two push mowers. The first time I had an accident was August 12, 1992 and I cut my foot. I started giving my yards away for the last three years I have about seven now in 1995.

Now, I get my Social Security and VA benefits. I don't have to work very hard now. But I try to stay in practice but is hard to do at the age of 76 years.

Part 2:

Road Trips

CHAPTER TWO

NASHVILLE

IN 2007, I took a group of senior citizens to Nashville, Tennessee. The group consisted of about 30 women and one man, my grandpa, whom you met in a previous chapter. By the way, his full name was Louis Van Montjoy, but most people called him "L.V."

Grandpa was a very funny man. He always had sayings or jokes that he could pull out of his hat. Well, my secretary of the group set up a reservation for us to have dinner and attend a live show while we were in Nashville. We went to see *Annie Get Your Gun*. We ordered our dinner, sat around, giggled and talked to one another for about 40 minutes; later, the show began.

Now if you're not familiar with the show, let me tell you a little about it. It's a Western musical loosely based on the life of sharpshooter Annie Oakley.

I remember it like it was yesterday. There was a scene where one of the actors pointed his rifle at my grandpa and Grandpa went straight down to the ground. Of course, we couldn't figure out why on earth he would drop to the floor. I looked at him and said, "Grandpa, get up! Why are you on the floor?" He said, "You never know, that rifle might not be unloaded." Then he goes on, "That's what happened to Bruce Lee's son. They thought the bullets were out of the gun and they weren't. That's how Brandon Lee died, by accident." As you've guessed, the gun was not loaded. I'm not even sure the gun was real, but you couldn't tell L.V. Montjoy anything when he saw that rifle pointed straight at him. Maybe he was having a flashback to when he was in the Army. All I could think of when he was lying on that floor was, "Wow! It would take an old man to think of that!

The next day it was time to head back to Sikeston, Missouri. I guess about 3 p.m. it was time to stop and get dinner. We stopped at this restaurant which was a smorgasbord. My grandpa loved the attention that he got from all the ladies. Miss Wilma Sue, who also went on the trip, was Grandpa's lady. Miss Wilma Sue was watching Grandpa and Grandpa had his eyes on another woman. He kept his eyes on Mattie John-son, who was a lot younger than Grandpa and had these extremely large breasts. So, as we took our seats, Miss Wilma Sue, decided she would get up and fix his plate. Meanwhile this guy Grandpa had met asked him, "What kind of group are you all?" Grand-pa explained to him who we were. The guy asked, "Are you the only guy in the group?" He says, "Yes, I'm the only rooster in this henhouse." He then says, "Man, you can talk to any of these women but two." He pointed to Mattie, then he started looking for Miss Wilma Sue. Seconds later, he felt someone pop him upside his head. Of course, he had no idea that Miss Wilma Sue heard the whole conversation.

I think that taught him a lesson at least for the time being: try not to bring up another woman when you're already with your woman! Considering he was an old man, you just let them get by with a lot. When people get older you realize they say the first thing that comes to their tongue without thinking. Plus, I'm convinced after spending so much time with older people that once they hit a certain age they deliberate-ly lose their filters!

CHAPTER THREE

ST. LOUIS, MO

O NCE AGAIN, in 2007 I decided I was going to take the *Senior Citizens On The Move*
to St. Louis Missouri. Of course, Grandpa
went along only this time it was two guys (him and
Mr. Shaw) and about 12 women. I gave each person a
food stipend of $50 for the one-day trip.

Now, St. Louis is about 120 miles north of
Sikeston. I promise you we could not have been on
the road 30 minutes before Mr. Shaw decides he's got
to use the bathroom. So, I pull over, he gets out, takes
care of his business, and we continue our trip. I drove
about 20 more miles when Grandpa decided he needed to go to the bathroom. I pull over trying to have
some patience with them, but they were wearing on
my last nerve! This happened at least two more times
before making it to St. Louis. Finally, I said, "I'm not

stopping anymore because we will never make it to St. Louis!" So, Grandpa says, "if you don't stop, I have a cup, and I don't know about the rest of them, but I will go if I need to." Honestly, at moments it felt like the scene from the movie *Are We There Yet?* Stop and go. Stop and go. Thank God we made it with no accidents and Grandpa didn't have to use that cup.

Once we got our rooms, and dinner, it was fun time. Mr. Shaw and Grandpa shared rooms. The women were paired two to a room. The guys had the only smoking room, and the rest of the rooms were non-smoking. Lillie Belle, Wilma Sue, Betty Mae, and I were playing cards in the lounging area outside the rooms. Here in the South we play a lot of Spades. Mattie comes out of her room wearing one of those lounging robes. She was walking slowly and, of course, when she walks that ample chest of hers just sticks right out. A lot of people these days have to pay for large breasts, but not her. Mattie stopped at the table and asked Miss Wilma Sue if it was all right if she went to L.V,'s room to smoke a cigarette. Miss Wilma Sue says, "That's fine with me, go ahead."

So, we continue to play cards. We were giggling and talking smack to each other while playing. If you play cards—especially Spades— then I know you understand what I mean about smack talking. We were playing, I guess for almost an hour or so, when we look up and see Mattie finally coming out of Grandpa and Mr. Shaw's room after smoking *only* one cigarette. She had a glow on her face and her walk was different. She became more perky and looked like she had gotten some energy from somewhere. We had forgotten she was in Mr. Shaw and Grandpa's room because she was gone for a good while.

Suddenly, Miss Wilma Sue says, "Hold up! What the heck you been down there doing? You went to smoke one cigarette and it took you that long? You got a new walk. What the heck? What have you been smoking?" It was so funny and we were laughing hard and loud. The security guard came up to our floor and told us that he had gotten some complaints that some senior citizens were extremely loud. He told us either to go to our rooms or we had to check out. That's a shame he was going to kick me and the little senior citizens out just because we were laughing. Seems like he and other folk in that hotel expected the seniors to be all shriveled up and quiet— not my group! Since none of us wanted to sleep in the van, we decided better just go back to our rooms still laughing at Mattie's glow. To this day, we still don't know what kind of cigarette she was smoking.

The next day it was time to check out. I called up the seniors to let them know I would be coming to their rooms to assist them. My roommate wasn't ready, so I grabbed my bag and went to go and get Grandpa and his bag. Grandpa and I made it to the elevator. I told him to stand right there beside the elevator and I would be back. I was going to go around the corner to help some of the other seniors with their bags. When I returned, he was gone. I panicked because I had no idea where he was, and I wasn't sure if he knew what floor we were on. So, I started to press the elevator buttons, determined to go to every floor to find him. Well, when the elevator doors opened, there he was! The conversation went like this:

"Grandpa, why did you get in the elevator?"

"You told me to get in the elevator."

"No, I didn't, I said stand *by* the elevator."

"Oh!"

"Did you get off on any of the floors?"

"No. I rode the elevator up and down, up and down because I wasn't about to get off until I recognized someone!"

I guess, he was a pretty smart guy.

CHAPTER FOUR

KANSAS CITY

IN THE summer of 2009, we decided to hit the road again. This time we did something different. We took an Amtrak ride to Kansas City, Missouri from St. Louis, Missouri. All the senior citizens were excited about this journey because no one had ever been on an Amtrak. Sure, most of them had been on a train that went town to town, but *not* an Amtrak.

I picked Grandpa up at 3 a.m. so we could drive to St. Louis. He told me he was so excited about the trip, that he hoped that I didn't forget to pick him up. Now how could I do that? Grandpa wanted to make sure he was ready; he told me he slept in his clothes. So, all he had to do was just get up and brush his teeth. I never thought to do that. Only the elderly. Thank the Lord we made it to the train.

It took us about five to six hours on the train to get to Kansas City from St. Louis. As we were riding the train, the conductor began to talk to Grandpa. He asked him several questions—that was right up Grandpa's alley because he loved to tell his stories.

Grandpa told the train conductor that he had a German Shepherd and her name was Girl. He went on that he was hoping his son had fed her. I guess he was missing her. He then proceeded to anyone listening just how smart she was. He even said he gave her a can of beer and the two of them would sit on the porch and drink together. I said, "Oh Grandpa, please!" He says, "Oh no, I'm serious!" This time there were other people that went on this trip besides the seniors. We had a friend on the train with us who is a psychiatrist. Dr. Bledsoe says, "Mr. Montjoy, you must mean you poured the beer in her bowl". Grandpa says, "No, she knows how to drink out of a can." The train conductor jumped in and said, "If he has a German Shepherd, I believe it, because those dogs are some smart dogs!" That little bit of agreement was all Grandpa needed to talk all the way to Kansas City!

Once we got to our hotel, Grandpa decided he was going to pretend he didn't know how to get to his room. (I guess there's an advantage to getting old). So, he played a dumb role. He saw these two pretty blondes and decided to play his card. They said, "Are you lost Mister?" He replies, "Yes. I'm confused on where my room is." Those ladies got on each side of him and helped him to his room. I guess he figured he would never have two women (especially white women) at the same time on his arms, so he might as well take advantage and be a lady's man even if only to get escorted to his room. I mean think about it, back in his day he might have gotten hung for just looking at one woman no less having one on each arm!

Later that night my sister, my aunt and I went by his room to check on him. He decided he wanted some coffee so my sister put some coffee on. When it was done, my aunt poured him a cup, but she realized he didn't have any sugar. She said "Mr. Montjoy, I will be back. I'm going to get you some sugar." He said, "Oh no, you can get it for yourself as for me I don't need any. All I have to do is stir with my finger because I'm sweet enough!" Only Grandpa!

CHAPTER FIVE

WASHINGTON, DC

O NE OF the members from the senior citizens group, Miss Bietrice, said we should visit the White House before President Obama got out of office. All I need from people is an idea sometimes and I will try my best to make it happen.

The fundraisers began so I could take the senior citizens on a trip to Washington, DC and hopefully also meet President Obama. We held fundraisers in January through April. We did things like plate lunches, selling candles, raffles, and even an all-you-can-eat pancake breakfast.

It's amazing how some people are so-called Christians. I will never forget I asked some so-called friends (or at least I thought they were friends) and I explained that I was selling breakfast tickets to help take a group of senior citizens to Washington DC to visit the White House. I also mentioned that I was praying we might meet the President. Well I guess that when I mentioned the President, I must have hit a nerve, because the so-called friend/Christians went off about how she wouldn't support anybody or anything that had to do with the President. She went on talking about her taxes and insurance she had to pay. Like it was our fault that she had those issues.

I have found out a lot of people are not who they pretend to be. So, after she got through basically saying she hated the President, I said, "I thought you were a Christian and I don't think it's appropriate for you to be hating anyone." I also told her that all she had to say was that she didn't want to buy any tickets. If you pay attention, God will reveal to you who people really are. People need to stop pretending to be Christians when they have hatred in their hearts. Stop it, please! That's all I have to say about that!

So, I had decided to get Grandpa one day. We were at my mom and stepdad's house. I asked Grandpa would he like to go to DC to visit the White House and possibly see President Obama. His eyes lit up and he said yes! Then he said, "Hold up, first of all, how are we going?" I said, "Grandpa we will be flying. He says, "Oh no! I'm not going to fly. I have never flown before. I said, "I know you have flown before. You were in the war and didn't you fly then?" He told me he didn't. He went over on a ship and came back to the States on a ship.

I told him it was 2012 and he needed to do something different and exciting. I told him he needed to make a bucket list. He said what is that? My mom says a list of things you want to do before you die. He looked at me as if we were crazy. He was quiet for about 30 seconds, and had a clap back by saying, "Listen, when you turn 90 years old and you lay down and wake up, that is exciting!" Mom and I burst out laughing and we said, at the same time, "That's true!"

After he thought about it and figured this was a chance of a lifetime trip, to see the only black president, he decided he better do it.

I was so excited because this was going to be the biggest trip I had ever taken the group on. A few nights went by and Grandpa called me one day and told me he had been up all night because he couldn't sleep. I asked him what was wrong. He had a conversation with someone who told him he had no business getting on a plane because he was too old and if he did go he would drop dead on the plane. That it was too risky. Why would it be risky when there is nothing wrong with him? He only takes blood pressure pills.

Some people have a lot of nerve, telling people cruel things. I always look out for the seniors. Also, my mom and Elder Pulley were going as well. Well, Grandpa didn't want any confusion, so he decided to back out of the trip. So, I just told him all about the trip and brought him back some souvenirs.

PRANK TIME

I decided to play pranks on the seniors as I always do. They fell for them all the time. Since I was the group leader I had access to everyone's room numbers. So, the night began with the first prank: I got up early the first day and called everyone at 5 a.m. for their courtesy wake up call. Yes, I know it seems cruel to wake folk up at 5 a.m. when they don't have to get up at that time, but it sure was a lot of fun!

That evening we decided to get up and travel to downtown Washington since our hotel was in Baltimore. We got on the train and had decided to pay for the Hop on Hop off trolley. Well when it was time to pay most of them decided they didn't want to spend their cash. We walked around the DC area instead. We visited several museums, the Capital, and we went to the mall as well.

The crazy thing is when you're from the South and you've never had the DC experience, it's funny. The reason I say that is we were looking for the mall. And a white man was telling us which Metro to get on, but the brother says," Nah, is not Red, get on the Green Line." So, the white guy is like, "I'm from here; it's the Red Line." We decided to follow his directions and we finally got off at the mall, and all we see is green grass, a monument and people walking around. We said," We thought we were going to the mall." He replies, "You're at the mall." Come to find out when you're in DC you have to say the *shopping mall* not the mall. It made me wonder if because the brother was a brother he knew we meant *shopping mall!* Lesson learned.

Finally, it was time to wrap it up and head back to Baltimore. After walking around for several hours, we got on the train and everybody in the group was very tired. It takes about 30 minutes on the train. The train began to cruise down the tracks, and the ride was so smooth until time went by and I dozed off. When I woke up, the whole group had fallen asleep. You wouldn't believe this, but we missed our stop to Baltimore. We panicked because we didn't know how to get back.

The train conductor was laughing, and he thought it was crazy that everyone went to sleep. He told us which train to get on and thank God, we didn't have to pay again. I'm glad to tell you that we made it back to the hotel in Baltimore and we all stayed awake to make sure we got there!

A lot of the seniors wanted to make it back for the free happy hour. So, we met downstairs, talked, ate, and drank margaritas. If it's free, the seniors are there!

The next morning, I decided to start phase 2 of the pranks by calling each room and pretending to be the front desk clerk and offering them a choice between Moscato and a fruit tray.

Sylvia and Wilma Sue

My first call was to Sylvia and Wilma Sue. Sylvia answered the phone.

"Hello"

"This is Victoria from the front desk. How are you?"

"Oh, I'm fine, besides my hip hurting and my feet hurt."

"Sorry to hear that. I want to let you know that for being a guest in our hotel you have the choice of a fruit tray or a bottle of Moscato.

"Oh, wow! Hold up. Let me ask my roommate."

"Okay.

"Ma'am, you still there?"

"Yes."

"Well, we would like the Moscato, but we two old women, and we're on a bunch of medication. And the pills may not work with the liquor."

"Ma'am, which one do you want?"

"Well I guess we may take the fruit tray."

"Okay, thanks."

Bietrice and Pauletta Jo

My second call was to Bietrice and Pauletta Jo. Bietrice answered the phone.

"Hello."

"This is Victoria from the front desk. How are you?"

"Just fine and you?"

"Great. I just wanted to let you know we will be giving you and your guest a fruit tray or Moscato for being a guest at our hotel, which would you like?"

(Screaming in the phone) "Hey, Pauletta Jo, it's the lady from the front desk. She wants to know if we want a fruit tray or Moscato. (Speaking to me) Please, can we get Moscato?

"Yes! Pink or white?"

(Yelling to Pauletta Jo again) "She wants to know white or pink? (Speaking to me) pink please."

"Okay, thanks.

Bridget and Cherry

The third call was to Bridget and Cherry. Bridget took the call.

"Hello."

"This is Victoria from the front desk, as you guys are guest at our hotel, you get to receive a fruit tray or a bottle of Moscato.

"We'll take the Moscato."

"Okay, white or pink?"

"Pink."

"Thanks."

Pastor Ronald Pulley and Murlee

My fourth and final call was to Pastor Pulley and his wife, Murlee. Unfortunately, no one answered the phone; however, I'm sure the conversation would have gone like this because Murlee (my mom) loves to try and compromise.

"Hello."

"This is Victoria from the front desk. Since you guys are guests at our hotel, you will receive either a bottle of Moscato or a six pack of beer.

"What is Moscato?"

"Champagne."

"We're Christians, and my husband is a pastor, and we don't drink."

"Oh, okay. So, you don't want anything?

"Is there any way we can have bottles of water instead?

"No. Your choices are Moscato or a six pack of beer. Do you want it or not, ma'am?'

"That's okay, because we don't drink alcohol."

"Okay. Thanks."

After I made all the calls—or maybe I should say playing on the phone, my roommate and I decided to go down stairs for breakfast. The seniors started coming in slowly. I told my roommate to follow my lead. I went to Patty first and told her that Victoria called my room and gave us a choice of a fruit tray or Moscato for bringing the group. Then one by one each person was like, "She called our room too!" At this point, my roommate was real close to bursting out laughing because she knew Victoria was me. It was hard to try to keep it together, but we managed.

I started acting like I was mad about the fact that they got the same offer I did. Right, I'm the one that did all the work and they didn't deserve the freebies. Pauletta Jo and Bietrice started snapping on me trying to remind that if it wasn't for them I wouldn't be on this trip. Then one of them says, "So you think you're better than us! Getting all swollen in the chest!"

Well, after they did all that talking, I told them, "By the way, you are not getting your fruit tray and you're not getting your Moscato." Yeah, the cat caught their tongue! Their bottom lips could have hit the floor. All of them said at the same time, "What are you saying?" I couldn't hold my laughter anymore and I said, "Yeah, I'm Victoria at the front desk. So, I got you all again. Bietrice says,

"So, you decided to bring us this far to trick us?"

"Yeah, gotcha again!"

The Strip Party Prank

I had a guy call and pretend he was on his way to their room for a strip party. This was hilarious! Patty answered the phone.

"Hello."

"Hello, is this room 1145"?

"Yes, it is. Why?"

"This is Sexy Chocolate, I just wanted to let you know I'm on my way up for the strip party."

"Excuse me?"

"I was told to come to room 1145 for the bachelorette party."

"Ooh baby, you must got the wrong room."

"No, I'm looking at my paperwork and I'm on my way."

"Look, now, I told you that you have the wrong room. Now Sweetie, if I had not have taken all of these pills, I would tell you to come on up. So, Sexy Chocolate, maybe another time".

(Laughing loudly) "Okay."

Senior citizens, once adults, twice the child. They say a lot of things that's on the tip of their tongues. Without any thought. That's one of the reasons why I love being with the group. You will find out a lot by being in their presence. Just make sure you're not easy to be offended!

CHAPTER SIX

HOT SPRINGS, AR

AS AFRICAN Americans, whenever we traveled, we tried to support African-American owned businesses. Unfortunately, we found out the hard way that sometimes we just couldn't 'do it.

Once we arrived in Hot Springs and checked our bags, our group decided we were ready for dinner. I went and asked the bellman, who was an African-American, about a great restaurant that he could recommend, and he did. Now, I'm not going to mention the name of the restaurant to protect the no-so innocent! Anyway, we got on the shuttle and headed to the restaurant.

When we walked in the restaurant, the server seated us and poured everyone a glass of water. He then gave us the menus. We noticed that after he took our orders and left that he never came back to see if we wanted anything else to drink. That was our first sign to leave, but we ignored it.

We waited for about 30 to 45 minutes...no food, no drink; and the buffet bar was empty as well. They didn't have any fried chicken, green beans, roast, I mean it was pretty much bare and what was there looked old. Still, some of us ordered the buffet and others ordered from the menu.

My mom, a very humble, respectful and soft talking lady, ordered from the buffet so she asked the owner, "Excuse me, sir, when will you have some more fried chicken?" The owner said, "It will be a little while, ma'am." Mom simply said okay.

We are now sitting for about an hour and 20 minutes... still no food or drinks. Yet, another sign that we should have gotten up and left! A little while had turned into 20 more minutes. My mom said, in her soft-spoken voice, "Excuse me, how much longer on the fried chicken?" The owner said, "Ma'am, look when the chicken is done I will let you know!" (It got so crazy until it became funny and we burst out laughing.) Meanwhile, we're still trying to give it a chance even though it felt like they kept lying saying the chicken was on its way. Now Mom's getting fed up. The server says, "I'm sorry but the cook don't feel like cooking today!" Wow!

Finally, those of us who ordered from the menu got our food after waiting about two hours. Some people in our group still didn't have their food and we had just enough of the foolishness, but we were. still trying to support this black business.

Miss Stephanie went to pay for her meal, even though none of us got a check. She pulled out a $100 bill to pay for her meal. (Let me remind you that it is about 9:30 p.m.) and the owner yells out in the middle of the restaurant, "Hey! Anybody got change for a hundred-dollar bill?" We all started looking at each other about ready to pass out from laughing so hard. I was expecting for some cameras to come out as if we were getting punked or something.

No one responded, and he actually told Ms. Stephanie that he didn't have change and she needed to borrow money from one of her friends to pay for her meal. She looked at him like he had just lost his mind, and said, "If you don't find no change, I'm not paying!" Some kind of way he got change.

Next up to pay her bill was my mom who never got her chicken. He asked her, "What did you get? She said, "Oh I'll tell you what I had. A little piece of chicken wing, a green bean, and a dash of mashed potatoes. Look, you never did fill up your buffet. The stuff I ate was old." I guess he had gotten fed up with her. He told her to just go ahead and don't worry about it. My mom would have rather had the food because she was hungry, plus she loves to eat.

When he got to me I decided to let him know about the 4-ounce ribeye that was supposed to be a 12-ounce ribeye.

"What did you have?

"I had a kid's meal ribeye because that was no 12-ounce steak and I definitely wasn't satisfied."

He said, "Give me eight dollars," and he fanned me out of the restaurant. Of course, that was really funny!

We all decided to get out of there. Don't worry, that was our last time and we would never recommend it as a place to eat in Hot Springs. We made it back to the hotel and the bellman asked us how it was. I said, "Horrible! We have to charge you for sending us there!"

The best thing Hot Springs has to offer is their hot tub baths and massages. There was a lady, about 95 years old, that went. She said it felt like they touched every bone in her body. That touches your heart when you know somebody really enjoyed themselves.

Yeah it was an adventure, but it was a great trip and I wouldn't change anything about it—not even the so-called soul food restaurant. I'm still trying to figure out how a cook don't feel like cooking!

CHAPTER SEVEN

ROBINSONVILLE, MS

WE HEADED to Robinsonville, Mississippi where the Seniors were hoping to hit the jackpot at one of the casinos! As we headed down 55 South from Sikeston, Missouri, we had about three vehicles trailing one another. Of course, I had to lead because the other drivers didn't know the way. When you have a carload of people and you're on a road trip you begin to talk, sing, and play games. I guess the folks who were in the Caravan were really talking. (Senior citizens, right?) When we exited off the interstate, I had to make a right turn when I got to the stop sign. The Caravan went straight through the stop sign. I'm looking through my rearview mirror asking the people in my car, "Where are they going?" So, I decided to call them, and Bietrice answered the phone.

"Hello."

"Hey, where are you all?"

"We're right behind you."

"I don't know who you are behind, but it's not me."

Bietrice burst out laughing as she tells the driver, "I think we're trailing the wrong car.

Edward, the driver says, "OMG, how on earth did that happen? He then asked, "Where are we?"

I told Bietrice, "I have no idea, but y'all need to turn around and figure out how to get to the store where we're sitting."

When you get a certain age, you may need to do less talking, and wear your glasses, so you know who you're trailing!

The senior citizens and I checked into the Veranda Hotel. I believe it's closed now, but it was absolutely beautiful. They were so excited to get to the casino, and they started moving faster than their normal snail speed. There's an old saying, "Money will make a person move." After this trip with the seniors to the casino, I know this to be true.

Edward and I decided to drop everybody off at the door, so they wouldn't have far to walk. As Edward and I parked, I noticed he still had another person in his van. He jumped out and yelled to me,

"Please tell her to get out!"

"Huh? What's going on?

"She ain't getting out."

"Ms. Carla, why won't you get out of the van?"

"I don't want to gamble."

"You don't have to gamble. We're about to eat at Paula Deen's restaurant first."

"Oh okay. He should've said that!"

Edward, who was about 70 himself, started walking and talking saying, "I can't see how you put up with the seniors!" Ms. Carla got out of the Caravan and remarks, "Oh my, I don't know if I can walk that far" to which Edward replied, "Oh well, you should've gotten out earlier, and I ain't driving you back to the front door!" Once again, once an adult and twice a child.

Finally, we went to the restaurant and I guess the seniors were really hungry (especially Ms. Sylvia) because Ms. Sylvia had fixed her plate so that it was at least 5 inches high. I don't know how she did that because the food never fell off the plate. Our server was worked half to death. He had about 15 people to serve at our table. They had that server getting everything they could think of. Poor Mohammed looked like he was getting tired of those folks. He was sweating and looking nervous, because when you're dealing with senior citizens they say some of the craziest stuff. They don't think about what they're going to say. Or how they're going to say it. You can only imagine, hold your breath and wait for it.

Now it's time to leave the tip. Everyone's hands started getting arthritis in them. They were so full and most of them didn't want to let go of the money to give the server a tip. Really? I told them they needed to send down at least two dollars each. I know how to count money, knowing I should have collected $30. Yes, you guessed it! I was short! This is what happens when it's time to unload the purse and the payers are all senior citizens. Lord have mercy! I also pray, Lord, please don't let me be that type when I become a senior citizen. These seniors are tighter than the screws in the Tennessee bridge! Well it was time to load up and go back to the hotel. Some decided to stay and gamble and that was fine. I guess they found a cure for that arthritis!

CHAPTER EIGHT

SOUTHHAVEN, MS

URING THE trip to Robinsonville, we had the unfortunate experience of having a medical emergency.

I went to my room, showered and got into the bed when my phone rang. It was about 9:30 p.m. and the caller informed me that one of my seniors had fallen and the ambulance was on the way. I jumped up, slipped my clothes on, and went downstairs. Patty was on the ground when I made it downstairs. I was trying to see about her while fighting some of the biggest mosquitoes I have ever seen. They were the size of a nickel! Thank God it didn't take long for the ambulance to come or else those mosquitoes would have carried us off to the next town.

After riding for about 20 minutes we finally made it to a hospital in Southaven, Mississippi. Now here's where the story gets interesting. Of course, I always thought if you were brought in an ambulance that you were priority, but not in this case at all. The EMT put Patty in a wheelchair in the ER, so we didn't think it would be long. Patty's leg and kneecap were twisted to the side and she was in a lot of pain while waiting. After about 30 to 40 minutes had passed, I went to the receptionist to ask how long it would be. She asked me if we had a number. I said, "What do you mean, a number? We came by ambulance and she is in a lot of pain." The receptionist snapped back, "Just about everybody who is here came by ambulance. Now you need to get a number and just wait." Wow, you gotta be kidding!

The nurse's aide came around the corner and yells, "Davis." We got excited and I said, "Here she is." The nurse's aide says, "I'm ready to take you to get blood work." Patty says, "Bloodwork for what? I'm here because I think my leg is broken." The nurse asked, "Are you Bette Davis?" Patty replies, "No, I'm Patty Davis." You won't believe the next thing to come out of that aide's mouth. Yes, she actually said, "My bad! Wrong person!" Really? Where do they do *that* at? This hospital!

The nurse informs us it will be a little while longer and

Patty and I both say at the same time, "OMG!" The time is going by and it is now about 12 a.m. She's still in a lot of pain; she's in tears by now. I went back to the front desk and asked how much longer it would be. The receptionist replied, and sarcastically I might add, "Whenever we get to your number we will call you." Clearly, the staff had not received any customer service training! So, I came up with what I thought was a great idea. I went back to Patty and said, "I have a plan." Patty says, "Okay, what is it, baby?" I said, "When I count to three I want you to scream and start holding your chest. Just do that and go along with me."

"Okay, baby

"One, two, three." (Patty is screaming and holding her chest).

I ran over to the receptionist, "Ma'am we need a doctor! She has a pacemaker and she must be in a lot of pain. Maybe something is wrong with her heart.

"Ma'am, didn't I tell you when we get to y'all's number, I will call you!

Unbelievable!

I told Patty that she did a great job, but it didn't work. We couldn't believe it, a hospital that goes by numbers and *not* emergencies.

Finally, about 5 a.m. our number was called. They took us to a room and put Patty in the bed. When the nurses moved her, she was in even more pain. A few minutes later, here comes the doctor and when we looked at him, I promise you, he looked like he had just gotten out of medical school. He examined her leg and said it wasn't broken, just swollen from the fall, then he left.

"Patty, he is too young. You need to ask for an old doctor because this guy doesn't look like he has enough experience to be a doctor.

"Girl, you know you're right! (laughing.)

This young boy, oops…doctor comes back in the room and tells Patty that she's fine and that he's going to discharge her. He even went as far as to say that after a couple of days the swelling should go down.

I could tell that Patty didn't feel comfortable with his diagnosis and she asked him "Well, why is my kneecap twisted to the side?"

He proceeds to tell her that it just looked like that but wasn't; it was just swollen. I'm pretty sure she didn't believe him and simply responded, "Yeah, I hear you."

We left the room and were getting ready to leave when Patty says she's got to go to the bathroom. I helped her as she walked to the bathroom using the crutches the hospital had given her. She went into the handicap stall and I asked her if she needed help, she said no. Minutes later, I heard a loud noise followed by Patty screaming, "Oh, help I can't get up." I went into the stall and some kind of way her body was lodged between two stalls. I ran out of the bathroom, yelling and screaming, "Help! Help!" The nurses ran into the bathroom to help her. Once they got her up, they told us that they couldn't let her leave until they rechecked her. It's about 8:30 a.m. now. We did not want to stay since we had been there since 10 p.m. the night before. Well, they convinced us to let them look at her again. They said, "You're going to have to get a number and we will be right with you." WTW?

So now it's time for me to just go off on this receptionist! The conversation went something like this.

"Why on earth do we have to get back in line? We haven't been gone five minutes."

"All I can say is at least you are the only ones here. You all are next. But we need to get all of your information again."

"That is just stupid. You've got the paperwork and it hasn't even been five minutes. Why can't you use the same paperwork?

"Because this is a different accident."

Really?

Lesson learned: never stop at this hospital in Southhaven…even if you think you're about to die. Keep it moving!

Part 3:

Senior

Moments

CHAPTER NINE

BEAUTY SHOP

G RANDPA LOVED coming to the beauty shop so I could shampoo his hair. He would call and ask if I had time to shampoo the squirrels out of his hair. In other words, his scalp was itching.

One day he asked my mom if she could cut his hair, and she did because she would do anything for him. After she cut his hair, he told her she had cut his hair like Kevin's dad from the *Young and the Restless*. That was Grandpa's way of saying that she cut too much off!

I believe he came to the beauty shop to be around the beautiful ladies. One thing about him was that he was definitely one of a kind. He could look at a person and he might not know that person, but after getting a little family history, he could tell them who they were kin to.

Grandpa had a friend named Carlos and he used to tell Carlos that there were two good men in Sikeston and it was him and Carlos! He didn't care who he said it in front of. I think the reason why he liked Carlos so much is because they were the only two men I knew who wore long sleeve button up shirts all year long – even in 100° weather. Both agreed that the long sleeves kept them from getting hot! They claimed it kept the heat off, so they actually stayed cooler. Go figure!

CHAPTER TEN

MOVIE NIGHT

ONE EVENING Grandpa was at Miss Wilma Sue's house. They were all cozied up on the couch watching a movie on TV. He started talking. Miss Wilma Sue called him Joy, and says "Joy, please stop talking so we can enjoy the movie." Now that was going to be pretty hard, because asking Grandpa not to talk was liking asking the sun not to shine.

So after about 20 minutes of being quiet, Grandpa looked over at Miss Wilma Sue and says, "I'm scared of you!" She took her eyes off the movie and said, "Why on earth would you be scared of me?" He said, "Because you killed off your exes. Your husband is dead and your other children's fathers are dead." Wilma Sue says, "It's not like I killed them; they just died."

That's what happens when you tell a talker to stop talking; they start thinking of a lot of silly things and sometimes they just say it! No filter...that was my Grandpa!

CHAPTER ELEVEN

FRIED GREEN TOMATOES

MISS WILMA Sue and Grandpa were pretty funny together. As a matter of fact, I think they were also great companions for each other. Grandpa knew a lot of people and they were crazy about him. Grandpa was 90 years old and he just loved having fun. He knew this other lady named Anna Belle, and they had dated before. Throughout the years they had kept in touch.

Grandpa never would hide anything from Anna Belle or Miss Wilma Sue. He would tell her every time Anna Belle called or came by. Miss Wilma Sue would tell Grandpa that when she was around she didn't want to hear about other women.

Ten minutes later he brings up Anna Belle's name again. At this point, Miss Wilma Sue was fixing him some fried green tomatoes. While slicing the tomatoes, she's getting pretty pissed off and cutting the tomatoes very hard. You could hear the knife hitting the table. He got real nervous then; he realized she was serious. Miss Wilma Sue says (as she is slicing the tomatoes) "Didn't I tell you don't be mentioning Anna Belle while I'm over here?" By now, she's about finished slicing the tomato and asked him, "Did you hear me?" Grandpa looked crazy then. I think he was trying to figure out what was going to happen next.

In his sweetest romantic voice, he says, "Wilma Sue, are you thinking about cutting me with that knife?" Miss Wilma Sue began to slice another tomato. With each slice she said, "I would"—then she sliced again—"never cut" — then she sliced again—"you in front" —then she sliced again—"of your grandchildren."

I think he may have gotten the point. Just don't mention another woman's name in front of another woman. Then Miss Wilma Sue made it real clear when she told Grandpa, "The only reason why I'm letting you get by with all of this drama is because you're old and all of your friends are dead. Now, hopefully you understand this time."

I'm not sure, but I think he learned *not* to mess with Miss Wilma Sue!

CHAPTER TWELVE

DOUBLE TROUBLE

ONE DAY Grandpa had a knock at his door; it was Miss Wilma Sue stopping by for a visit. He loved to sit at the kitchen table drinking several cups of coffee every day. Grandpa's favorite spot in the house, hands down, was the kitchen.

As they sat there talking, laughing, and drinking coffee, there was another knock at the door. Miss Wilma Sue was looking at Grandpa -like, I wonder who is that? Grandpa opens the door, and there's his other lady friend, Anna Belle. He started to get a little nervous having two of his lady friends in the house at the same time. Of course, Anna Belle knew that Miss Wilma Sue was over there, because she saw her car outside. Grandpa invited her into the kitchen and asked her if she would like some coffee. Now you know she said yes.

When Miss Wilma Sue sees her coming into the kitchen, she decided to scoot over and sit in the next chair. Since Anna Belle was a little heavier, I guess Miss Wilma Sue figured that it would be pretty tough for Anna Belle to squeeze through. Anna Belle thanks Miss Wilma Sue. But you can feel the tension with Grandpa (one man) trying to figure out what on earth was about to happen with these two women sitting at his kitchen table. Anna Belle decided to start with some small talk.

"How have you been doing L.V.?"

"Oh, I'm doing pretty good. What about you?"

"I'm glad you asked. I'm better now that I'm here with you."

Meanwhile, Miss Wilma Sue is sitting there looking as if she wanted to slap both of them—while Anna Belle continues her conversation with Grandpa.

"You know, L.V., my nephew's wife has been running around on him. I can't stand her."

Anna Belle started calling her niece-in-law all kinds of bad names. Miss Wilma Sue was in a state of shock because she had no idea that Anna Belle cursed like that.

L.V. was just looking like, "Oh my God, she is cursing." Anna Belle went on and on with all the name-calling. After she finally finished, she told Grandpa she was leaving and that she would call him later. He says okay. Anna Belle leaves and shuts the door a little hard. Okay, she slammed it!

Well, I don't have to tell you, but Miss Wilma Sue was steaming! She says to Grandpa "Hey, Joy, well, I had no idea that Anna Belle cursed like a drunken sailor." Grandpa drops his head and has a smirk on his face. Miss Wilma Sue says "Joy! Does she curse like that all the time?" L.V started shaking his head no. Then he finally raised his head up.

It didn't take Miss Wilma Sue long at all to figure out that Anna Belle's name-calling and bad talk was meant for her. She screamed, "Joy, you better never let me find out she was actually talking about me. It's mighty funny she started cursing today of all days. When I find out I'm going to get both of you!"

I'm pretty sure that Grandpa wished a thousand times that he had never answered that second knock because it seems like all it got him was double trouble!

CHAPTER THIRTEEN

GIRL

ONE MORNING I got a strange phone call from Grandpa. He didn't sound like himself. His dog, Girl, had been sick. The German Shepherd belonged to one of Grandpa's late sons who was murdered back in 2001, and Grandpa had the dog from birth. I'm not sure of the dog's age, but whatever it was, the dog and my grandpa were the same age—90 years old.

Grandpa told me he was getting nervous, because Girl had passed away. He felt like his time was getting close as well because he and Girl were the same age.

Grandpa had a little humor for everything, even dying!

CHAPTER FOURTEEN

DISTURBING NEWS

I HAVE never understood why some people love delivering bad news to people. It's like they want to be the first one. Grandpa had already been dealing with the death of his wife, three sons, and one daughter. That's from 1992 through 2012—almost too much to bear.

He had a daughter who was battling with cancer for several years. God had given her breath when the doctors thought she was taking her last one. Auntie had been in the hospital for several days. People kept putting out fake news that she had died before she actually died. This is typical — folks!

So about 3 a.m. Grandpa gets a call that his daughter had passed away. Later that day, I called Grandpa and asked him if he would like to go to the hospital to see his daughter.

"No."

"Why not? She would love to see you."

"How is she going to see me if she is dead?"

"Dead? She's not dead, but she is very sick."

"Yes, please come and get me."

I went to pick him up and when he got into my car, he said he had been up since 3 a.m. and he had no idea why someone would call and tell him his daughter was dead when she wasn't. It had really gotten to him and I could see the sadness all over his face.

We made it to the hospital, so we could see Auntie. Grandpa went to the side of her bed. He looked at her with tears in his eyes. He knew it wouldn't be too long before God would be coming for her. She looked at him and said, "Daddy, I love you." Of course, he told her the same. He started walking out of the room. Auntie looked at me and said "Tonya, do you think Daddy will outlive all of his kids?" Then my eyes watered up and I said, "I don't know!" We said our last goodbyes, and when we got in the car Grandpa said that he wasn't going to stick around to bury any more children.

CHAPTER FIFTEEN

CHICKEN POT PIES

L.V. MONTJOY loved to eat chicken pot pies. One day his oven stopped working which meant no more chicken pot pies. I told him that I would go and get him another one, but he told me he didn't need another stove. I told him that the stove looked pretty old; he said it was. In fact, the stove was over 50 years old. Grandpa told me he didn't need a stove because he wasn't going to stick around to use it

"What do you mean, Grandpa?"

"I'm going home!"

"Grandpa, you're at home now."

"No. I am going home to be with my wife."

I don't know about you, but I didn't really want to hear Grandpa talking like that. The conversation about Girl dying was still on my mind and now this.

About five months later, he ended up having to get one of his legs amputated because he was a smoker. Even though his other leg needed to be amputated they only removed one at that time. It was the big day; the nurse came in and got him ready for surgery. He looked up and said, "One day you have both legs, and when you close your eyes and open them again you're one leg short." He knew how to share laughter even at bad times.

CHAPTER SIXTEEN

NO PARTIES

YOU KNOW the doctor said if he didn't have the other leg removed he may not live past two or three months. I believe a lot of times the doctors give people hope when they really know it doesn't make sense to have surgery. He didn't have the other leg amputated and he still only lived for about two months anyway.

Grandpa had said he didn't want any more birthday parties. He had a good friend, Sister Sarah, who had a big 90th birthday party. She had been waiting all year for her party. Finally, Sister Sarah had her party and she was so happy and excited about it. Well, God called her home within a month after her party. That's why Grandpa didn't want us to throw him a party. He said, "I don't want any more parties. If I have to have a party and then just turn around and die, just forget it! That was L. V. Montjoy for you. Always a reason for something.

So, on April 26, 2013, Grandpa's children threw a barbecue for his birthday, which is on April 27. They had quite a few of people over that day. I went into his room and he was just sitting there in his wheelchair looking very lonely. I asked him if he was okay, and he said yes. But he was tired and wanted to go outside. I pushed him outside and sat there with him for a little bit. Lord knows I had no idea my goodbye was going to be the last one.

The next day, Sunday, April 27, I got that phone call. My sister was crying and saying, Grandpa just died, he died exactly where he loved to be — in his house at the kitchen table. So even though it was sad for us, what a way to celebrate your birthday by going home to be with the Lord.

I will always believe that people have some type of feeling that they know that they are going to die. They don't know exactly when and what time, but somehow, they can feel death is close.

I shall never forget all the great times and trips that we shared. I loved my Grandpa with all my heart!

Part 4:

Lessons

CHAPTER SEVENTEEN

WHY SENIORS?

I ESTABLISHED *Senior Citizens on the Move* around 2003. It started off with about six seniors and it grew to about 15 to 20 people, which was enough people for one person to look after. I decided to start this group because no one in my area was doing anything for the seniors. They have worked hard all their lives, so it was time to show them how much they were loved. Besides that, they deserved to have a little fun.

We didn't receive government money like a lot of the organizations did, so we had to do a lot of fundraisers for every trip we took. We did different things in the community:

- Full Figure Fashion Shows
- Men's Fashion Shows

- Back-to-School Fairs
- Health Fairs
- Pageants
- Christmas Programs
- Halloween Harvest Parties
- Mother of the Year, and many, many more.

I have enjoyed hearing stories from a lot of the seniors. They were my heart and I enjoyed every trip. And as you read earlier in this book, I always came back with some good stories.

So, we must remember if your heart isn't in something, don't start it. I did this for 13 years with no pay at all because it was from my heart. We met once a month at a local church, then we started meeting at my house. We would play games and we always had a meal prepared. I could tell that my older crew of seniors loved it as much as I did. The original crew did a lot of the work and really showed me love.

As time went by, my grandpa started going downhill. He was one of my original members and was very faithful to the group. So, once he got out of the group at the age of 90, it didn't seem the same. We also used to collect dues each month and sometimes Grandpa would be a gentleman and pay someone else's dues.

That day came when God called him home, then pieces of my heart left. I'll always have the seniors in my heart and I thank those who really did have my back.

CHAPTER EIGHTEEN

DRIVING THE BUS

G RANDPA HAS to be the only person I know that drove a bus, and had a switch laying in front of the windshield. Now, if you don't know what a switch is, let me explain…it's a small limb from a tree—old school discipline.

One of his students named Ken told me that Grandpa and Mr. Moore, another bus driver, used to race each other to the school. The kids on Grandpa's bus would cheer him on to beat Mr. Moore pulling up to the school. Once, Grandpa cut across the grass just to beat Mr. Moore. I still haven't figured out how anyone didn't get hurt.

A lot of people thought Grandpa had retired from driving a school bus, including me. Grandpa told me he was fired from the school system. He said that they found empty beer cans on his bus. They said they needed to know if he was drinking and driving. Grandpa told them that he drank six in the morning and six in the evening. Then he said, "With those bad-tail kids you have to drink something." The people at the school said it was against the law to be drunk while driving. Grandpa said he was never drunk. The school told him it didn't matter because he couldn't drink and drive. He was an honest man because he could have lied. As he said, "Always tell the truth." He lived by that.

Grandpa said one of the best days of his life was the day they fired him. After that he started mowing yards, and he was making up to $350 per week in yard work.

When he did drive the bus, there weren't too many times when he would wait for the children to make it to the bus stop. If he did wait, they had to be pretty special. He expected them to be there when the bus got there and not running down the road trying to catch it. To him, that meant they had no respect for time and he was always about time in his schedule. He wanted to teach the children that the world didn't revolve around them. I think a few may have learned that lesson, but I can only hope.

FAMILY LOVE

RANDPA WAS so heartbroken especially after his second daughter passed away. Before she got sick, she would do all she could—anything within her power to help him. She would make sure things were done. When it was time for Grandpa to go out of town with me, she would have his bags packed. She always made sure she took him food as well. Grandpa appreciated everything she did for him and so did I.

Another one of his daughters moved back to Sikeston because she was ill. Grandpa was so happy to have her around and he helped take of her. He would take her to the doctor, to the grocery store— whatever he could do, he would do. He even decided that he wasn't going to go over one of the trips because he was worried about her. Love will make you do things you can't imagine.

For me, seeing these things was a testimony of how love works in families. When we are young, our parents take care of us; when they are old, sometimes we take care of them. It's like a circle of love that keeps families together, especially when things get rough.

I'm blessed to have been a witness to the love that flowed from Grandpa to his children and from his children to him.

CHAPTER TWENTY

LOSING LOVED ONES

IN this chapter I want to talk briefly about growing old and losing the people you love.

In 1997, Grandpa lost his wife which was devastating to him. They had been married for 47 years and were the parents of twelve children. I think people can feel that death is coming, but they have no idea when and where it's going to happen. I know that sounds crazy, but I'm a firm believer. Near the end of her life, I was able to spend some quality time with Grandma. In fact, I saw more of her in the last six months of her life than I had in very long time. Grandma passed away peacefully, but that doesn't mean it still didn't hurt Grandpa to lose his life-long companion. To my knowledge she wasn't sick; she died in her favorite chair with the Bible in her hand.

I've heard my seniors say more than once that no parent should have to bury their child. Well, Grandpa ended up burying five of his twelve children. He lost two sons to murder, and one son and two daughters to sickness.

As if that wasn't enough, he received a call about one of my younger cousins who was Grandpa's grandson. He had surgery on his hip but ended up having a blood clot. He fell as he was trying to get up out of the hospital bed. I don't need to tell you, he ended up dying as well. He was Grandpa's first grandson. It bothered Grandpa so much he couldn't bear to even attend the funeral service. I can see him now, shaking his head and eyes full of tears.

I sometimes wonder if losing so many loved ones just didn't break Grandpa's heart.

CHAPTER TWENTY-ONE

MANY NAMES

OVER DECADES even though he was one person, Grandpa was a guy with many names: L.V., Pops, Grandpa, Grandfather, Granddad, Poppa, Louis, Brother Montjoy, Paw-Paw, Joy. This is what happens when you're loved by so many people.

I think through his journal entries and the stories, you can see that my grandpa was honest, talkative, trustworthy, funny, a people person, and educator, father, brother, grandfather, uncle, unpredictable, survivor, hard worker, and very handsome. He met so many people in his 94 years of life.

He loved to travel and loved meeting new people. I wish he had been able to meet President Barack Obama. Grandpa grew up in a time when no one could imagine that a black man would become President of the United States of America. I think for Grandpa and folk like him, living long enough to see that may have eased some of the injustices they had to deal with: Jim Crow, prejudice, sharecropping, and having to sit on the back of the bus. Maybe it helped him feel like his living was not in vain.

Trust me, if we keep living maybe we will be half the person he was because Grandpa was a great man and his character spoke for itself.

CHAPTER TWENTY-TWO

FINAL THOUGHTS

I THINK a good way to wrap this up is to tell you what I've learned from my wonderful group of senior citizens. Maybe it will help you understand the senior citizens in your life a little better.

- Cherish your family and friends. When people get older, family and friends mean even more than ever. I know…you're busy but make time to swing by and check on Sister Annie Mae, fix a meal for Auntie and stay while she talks your ear off probably telling you the same thing over and over.

  If you need to take care of a parent, remember that they don't want to be a burden to their children. We, as the younger generation, should always be there for them. Instead of asking a parent to move in and tiptoeing around, make them feel comfortable.

- Remember, if you live long enough you're going to be a senior citizen one day, too! As you get older and older, you realize nothing remains the same. So, don't fret about those extra pounds or the wrinkles and the sags. Love yourself!

- Give people sincere compliments. You like to hear nice things and so do seniors. Just taking time out to let someone know how pretty they look, or even maybe how good their hair looks will put a smile on their face. Listen, seniors get it and they already know that they don't look the same, but they're not dead either. They want to feel beautiful and handsome like the hot fox they used to be.

- Be honest with yourself about yourself, whether it's good or bad. In some kind of way, history repeats itself. You're not perfect and that's okay.

- Stand up for yourself. Our seniors stepped up to the plate on not having to settle for things. For example, when you go to a restaurant and the food is horrible and you receive poor service, don't settle, stand up for what's right.

- See as much of the world as you can. A lot of the seniors may be hopping, but they ain't stopping and they want you to learn early that there's a big world out there and you should see it. Get out of your comfort zone! Several of my seniors had opportunities to go and visit places they had never been before. They figured you only come through this world one time, so why not see it and enjoy it?

- Learn to be patient, especially with seniors and try to understand their decisions. Maybe they don't want to walk through a casino because it brings back bad memories. Perhaps their dad or mom was a gambler. Maybe the reason why they don't like driving is because they were in a bad car wreck when they were younger.

- Appreciate the opposite sex! Seniors definitely love the attention from the opposite sex. Don't let a handsome young guy walk by an older lady trying to carry her bag. Suddenly, she doesn't have strength at all. Yep! They want to hear, "Do you need any help, Ma'am?"

- Learn to shut down useless noise. When they don't want to be bothered with you, they pretend their hearing aid isn't working—even though they don't have a hearing aid! What they're doing is shutting down conversation that's not important to them. Sometimes we put up with and listen to stuff that is negative and hateful. Take it from the seniors, make sure your hearing aid isn't working!

- Just because you're getting older doesn't mean you have to look old! Thank God for Miss Clairol (hair color).
- When your hair starts to thin out, remember that nothing remains the same...get yourself a beautiful wig.

Like I said earlier, if we live long enough we, too, will be a senior citizen one day. Just remember that being a senior has a lot of advantages:

1. When you don't feel like walking someone can push you in a chair.
2. You don't have to stand in the long airport lines.
3. You receive discounts.
4. No more babysitting (you're just too old)!
5. People chauffeur you around.
6. If you see the opposite sex and they look good, you can pretend you need a little help.
7. You can say whatever you want to say, and people will just blame it on your age.

8. You know all the history. Everybody may have thought Billy and Betty were cousins, but you know that Billy and Betty are really siblings!

As a wise senior citizen once told me, "I'm not old, the reason I look like this is because I've just been around a little longer."

May you love the seniors in your life and stay around a little longer to become one yourself one day!

ABOUT THE AUTHOR

Tonya Mitchell founded and operated *Senior Citizens On The Move*, a group formed to give seniors citizens a positive outlet. This strictly volunteer organization was an active part of the community for more than 12 years. The City of Sikeston presented her with a Gold Key for her leadership in her community. She also served as a community liaison for St. Louis University of St. Louis, Mo. Ms. Mitchell has a deep love for all seniors and has always clicked with the elderly.

She graduated from Sikeston Senior High School in Sikeston, Mo., and then attended Ser's Beauty College in Charleston, Mo. where she received her Cosmetologist license.

Ms. Mitchell is the proud mother of two daughters: Tyianna Bonner Davis and Tyra Bonner. She is also a doting grandmother to Dorion Jr and Brooklyn.

Tonya loves to travel and has seen quite a bit of the world. One of her life goals is to visit every state in the United States.

To book Ms. Mitchell contact her at:
booktonyamitchell23@yahoo.com

www.ingramcontent.com/pod-product-compliance
Lightning Source LLC
Chambersburg PA
CBHW060323070426
42446CB00049B/2014